"Broke Every Branch on the Way Back Up"

by Josh Adcock

Trigger Warning! Contains Poetry.

Broke Every Branch on the Way Back Up.

© 2025 Josh Adcock

Broke Every Branch on the Way Back Up

All rights reserved. No part of this publication may be reproduced, stored in a retrieval system, or transmitted in any form or by any means — electronic, mechanical, photocopying, recording, or otherwise — without the prior written permission of the author.

This is a work of creative nonfiction. Names, places, and experiences may have been adapted, exaggerated, or entirely imagined. Mental health is complicated. So is poetry.

First edition, 2025

Printed by Amazon KDP

Broke Every Branch on the Way Back Up.

Dedication:

This book is dedicated to the struggle —
to those living in it,
those who've felt it,
those who visit it on occasion,
those affected by it,
those who've succumbed to it,
and those who dedicate their lives and careers
to bringing light back.

It's also dedicated to my son, Leo —
the reason I'm still here.

Broke Every Branch on the Way Back Up.

Warning: Contains emotion, feelings, naughty words, breakdowns, realisations and anger.
Mostly disguised by humour or buried beneath sarcasm.

Broke Every Branch on the Way Back Up.

Introduction:

I pick my humour from the dark —
Because I've lived it,
and that's why I'm still here.

This book isn't polished, perfect, or sugar-coated.
It's a mix of anger, honesty, depression, awkwardness,
swearing, anxiety, neurodivergence, accidental raves, and
unapologetic individuality.

It's a book about coping —
mostly through jokes,
sometimes through swearing,
and often through saying what most people are too polite to
admit.

Some of this might make you laugh.
Some might hit too hard.
Some might offend you.

That's fine.
I didn't write it to be safe.
I wrote it to be real.

If you've ever felt broken, stupid, lost, angry,
or like you're one bad moment from snapping —
This book is for you.

And if none of that applies to you…
then I hope you enjoy it too, you lucky, jammy bastard.

Broke Every Branch on the Way Back Up.

About the Author.

Josh Adcock writes from his heart, from his soul, and from his frantic, fucked-up brain. When neurodivergence, depression, and comedy collide, this is the result: a collection that's raw, relatable, and occasionally unhinged. He blends dark humour with uncomfortable honesty — mainly because it's cheaper than therapy.

He doesn't claim to be a professional poet. He just survived some things, overthought others, and decided to slap it all onto a page. This is his first book. He never thought he'd finish one. But here it is.

Broke Every Branch on the Way Back Up.

Contents:

9. Almost positive thinking.
10. ADHD IMDb.
12. Like... Hello?
13. Neurodivergent problems.
14. Lunchtime.
16. Bum hole, dragon cocks.
18. Reflection.
19. ADHD scheduling.
20. Please don't fall.
21. Rice cakes and bullshit.
22. Noise.
24. Mortal enemy.
25. Do sheep get heavier in the rain?
26. Box theory.
27. I wonder what it is?
28. Neuro Domino.
29. Cunts.
30. Reaching.
31. Plancellation .
33. Plancelled on.
34. Request Pending.
35. The scenic route.
36. Don't give up giving up.
37. Suicidal sympathies.
38. Forty.
39. Dead tired.
40. When the mask is broken.
41. Proverb problems.
42. The place.
43. Just a word.
44. Boulders.
46. Sweet restraint.
47. Listening, not hearing.
48. Give him a chance.
50. Riding the darkness.
51. The voice.
52. I cried today.
54. Meanwhile, Dave....
55. The cats eyes.
56. The ADHD control room.
58. I'd like to take my brain out.
60. The persistent optimist.
61. Grief is a funny old thing.
62. Life.
64. Thank you.
65. Talk to someone, anyone.
66. Eulogy.
67. I tried.
68. The Tree.
70 Flipped!
71. Afterwards.
72. Hard to explain.
74. If you're struggling - helplines.

Broke Every Branch on the Way Back Up.

If You're Struggling.

If you find yourself struggling in silence — please know you're not alone. Life can be unbearably heavy sometimes. I've been there, and I know how loud the quiet can get.

Asking for help isn't weakness — it's survival. It's strength in the rawest form.

If you're in the UK and need someone to talk to, here are some places you can reach out to:

- **Samaritans – 116 123 (free, 24/7)**

- **Mind – 0300 123 3393 or text 86463 (Mon-Fri, 9am-6pm)**

- **SHOUT – Text 'SHOUT' to 85258 (free, 24/7)**

- **NHS Mental Health Helpline – Call 111 and press option 2**

Wherever you are, search for mental health helplines in your country — someone will be there. Someone will listen. You matter.

Take care of your weird, wonderful self.

Almost positive thinking

Attention to small details and desire for perfection.
Innovative, resilient, an expert in deflection.
Good at working as a team, creative problem solving.
Adapts to tasks quicker than most, brain constantly evolving.

Blends in like a chameleon, a wearer of a mask,
Enhanced creativity, will take on any task!
These are neurodivergent traits, but just the good details.
For every good there's 2 bad ones. It really tips the scales.

"It's like having super powers they say and if they could they'd choose it"

But what good's a fucking super power when you can't be arsed to use it?...

ADHD IMDb.

"Let's watch a film, let's watch a film, what film dya wanna watch?"
I'm jumping round the living room like I'm doing the hopscotch.

"Maybe something easy? A musical or comedy?"

"Nah I want an action film with Stallone in or Bruce Lee"

"Ok then why'd you ask then if you've practically decided?"

"I thought you couldn't decide babe, you're practically divided"

"Ok love if you want action, how about big guns 6?"

"Yeah that one sounds good and will increase my dopamine fix"

"Who's that guy, what's he been in? I've seen that bloke before?"
"Oh that's right he played the chap from 'boom' in ninety four"
"He was also in 'space monkeys', I didn't know that was him"
"And in that film called 'Wet World' he's the one who couldn't swim!"

"He was born in south London, wow I thought he was a yank"
"He's 6ft 6 babe, bloody hell. The blokes built like a tank"
"That's her from that tv show, the one about the farm"

"For fuck sake babe I'm tryna watch! You need to be more calm!"

"The twist at the end was fantastic, an instant classic thriller!"

"Why what happened I missed it? Look, high score on Zombie Killer…"

Like... Hello?

Can't you see I'm driving here you cut me up you prick!
Yeah I was doing 90 but you're still a fucking dick!

Oi mate he pushed in, I was next, come over here and serve!
So what if you didn't see me maaan, you've got some fucking nerve!

Did you not see my trolley, aimed with purpose down the aisle?
You parked yours blocking everyone, don't give me that rueful smile.

You stepped out that shop brazenly, I had to hit the brakes!
Doesn't matter if I'm riding on the path or not, fuck sake!

It's not hard to move a trolley if you push it with your own.
But doing so with cars is something I can not condone..

Take a breath and accept that some people are just twats.
Even if we probably could have avoided all that....

Neurodivergent problems.

I'm waiting for my food to cook there's 2 minutes to go.
That's not a lot of time to wait. Why does it seem so slow?
I'd better stay right here though or I'll miss the oven beep.
No time to wipe the surface down, no time for me to sweep.
So how come when eventually the alarm starts to sound,
I'm in the fucking shower, or nowhere to be found?...

Lunchtime!

Is that the time already? It's twenty five to two!
Time flies when you're avoiding doing things you need to do.
I'll crack on with the chores and stuff when I've had some lunch.
I forgot to eat again, no breakfast or no brunch!

I've got to paint the garage door and drop that thing at mums,
I was gonna make a sandwich but all I could find was crumbs.
I'll go and check the freezer, is there any bread in there?
It's outside in the garage though, oooh what shoes shall I wear.

Those will do, two left shoes, I won't be in them long,
No idea at all where the opposite shoes have gone..
Ok I'll pop my shoes on then and head out to the freezer.
I'd better take this paint out too, well remembered geezer!

I swear I left my keys just here? At least I normally do.
Maybe in my joggers? There they are, let's look through.
Good example of why I leave my washing lying around.
Here's the keys, oooh and I've just found a pound!

What was it I was doing? What am I upstairs for?
Oh go away!! Not now, the bloody postman's at the door.
Oh Shit bread I'd better get some out the garage quick.
It's half past 3 already? OUCH there's that missing Lego brick.

Right I'm in the garage, wow this place is a mess.
I'd better give it a really quick tidy up I guess
My bike is in the way here and the tire has gone flat.
I meant to get a new tyre, I'll just take care of that.

BREAD! I was looking for bread. Let's open the freezer lid.
Fuck sakes I've not got bread in here, I could've sworn I did!
Right back to the drawing board, what shall I have for lunch?
It's 4pm, it's dinner time...

Fuck it. Monster munch..!

Bum hole, dragon cocks.

Words are used by all of us, language is took for granted,
Speaking is a skill that once you've learnt becomes implanted.
The simplest task for most of us, combine our mouth and brain,
Use it to communicate, give orders or complain.

The beauty of some words are that some hold colossal power,
What impact would it have if you shout "CUNT" off Blackpool tower?
Just like fuck, twat, shit and piss it's a four letter word,
But the way people react to cunt whenever it is heard,

Some will find it hilarious, others sadly not.
You'd think someone had punched their dog with how irate they got.
You can go to Tesco and walk up to the cashier.
And whisper "bum hole, dragon cocks" then swiftly disappear.

They're gonna think you're mental which I suppose you should expect..
But it was just 4 simple words, not a proper dialect.
You can physically say to someone anything at all,
But the different choice of words could crack a smile or start a brawl.

2 sentences, 4 words in each just as a demonstration,
Will show a total contrast of resentment or elation.
If you approached a person and tried out your sentences.
You'll get a perfect understanding of what consequence is.

"Morning fella, lovely hat" would probably make him smile.
"You look a cunt" hits differently, it can turn someone hostile.
Next consider words that could get you in heaps of shit.
They check your bag at customs, you say "there's a bomb in it"

Approaching Tyson fury to say "I've just bummed your gran"
You really start to see how things get quickly out of hand.
So think about the impact of your words when they are spoken.
Avoid saying the things that could get your nose freshly broken.

Say something nice to someone you don't know, every day.
You never know it may just be the highlight of their day

Reflection.

I saw my own reflection in a shop window today.
I try to avoid looking, in the hope it goes away.
It serves as a reminder of the setbacks in my life,
Every failed accomplishment — it cuts just like a knife.

A mirror of my failures with savage tenacity.
Callous with its attitude, bold audacity.
Laughing at me viciously from the safety of its realm,
Gaslighting me relentlessly while steering at the helm.

"Sort your life out," it insists, "get some self-respect!"
It grinds me down to nothing, then laughs when I'm a wreck.
But this time things were different — I refused to bow my head,
Refused to cower to its wrath, dismissed the slurs it said.

I smiled and winked defiantly, this time they bowed their head.
We both knew now I was in charge, whatever lies ahead.

ADHD scheduling.

"Brain, cancel my 3 o'clock, I've got something more pressing.
I moved that thing from yesterday whilst I was busy stressing.
I know I moved that thing twice now, that's why I need to do it.
Just move the other thing to tomorrow, we'll get through it.

It doesn't matter that I have already got loads on.
We can slip this small thing In, just move our thing with Jon?
I know it's been a long time since I finished all my things,
It doesn't mean I'll keep doing it, see what tomorrow brings.

A few more things in a list of things isn't much extra stress.
We'll jiggle about other things, it's like a game of chess.
Look, I moved my thing last week and I finished it yesterday,
So all the things we're moving now will all go the same way!

Shit that thing from Monday that I moved needs doing too.
Oh fuck it, put the kettle on, let's have another brew.

Please don't fall.

Have you ever felt like you can't go on, like nothing even matters?
Have you ever felt totally numb, your soul ripped into tatters.
Have you ever reached the point where you don't ask why, but how shall I end it all?
Have you ever realised that you don't need to be alone?

Please. Don't. Fall.

Rice cakes and bullshit.

"Pain is weakness leaving the body" a bloke once said to me.
In between reps and protein shakes with mounds of creatine.
"It depends whose pain you're on about" I replied pleasantly.
"My pain is kind of a mental thing, with more complexity.

And whilst you see it differently, this discussion at hand,
You're basing your advice on something you don't understand!
Pain isn't weakness, not one bit, it's a feeling of emotion.
It's something you can't help to feel when it sets its wheels in motion.

If you use it egotistically to make out someone's weak,
It makes you a massive cunt, your future's looking bleak.
So enjoy your fish and rice cakes, and thanks for the advice,
But fuck off you gormless, caveman prick, don't make me tell you twice."

Noise.

Down the pub one day I saw the wife began to growl.
Shit! Operation Hangry! – I felt it in her scowl!
I leapt into action, grabbed menus and ordered grub.
I dealt with that amazingly, I was feeling pretty smug.

But as I looked up gloating, it was obvious to see,
I'd done something wrong? Oh no! What could it be?
"Are you for real? Did you hear a single word of that?"
But she's the only one who knew we were having a chat!

"I'm sorry I zoned out again I'm always doing it"
"Probably weren't important tho, you're always chatting shit.."
The first bit that I said was fine, honest and apologetic..
Then next I should have followed up with something more poetic..

But 9 times out of 10 my mouth works faster than my brain,
And I wonder why I said something so stupid yet again.
She knows deep down inside that I didn't really mean it,
The excuse I used, I've used before which then tends to demean it.

I'm now digging a bigger hole whilst trying to explain,
It's hard keeping up when you've got such a busy brain.
But she doesn't hear that lady eating whilst she talks,
Or the lady in the kitchen sorting out the knives and forks,

The till drawer swinging open, causing the clash of change.
The bloke playing the bandit is just audibly in range.
There's a baby crying loudly in the bar area too.
You've fed her and she's just woken, it's blatantly a poo!

There's kids running about the place and they're unsupervised.
If it was up to me the noisy twats would be chastised.
Then once again I've strayed away from the point at hand.
I'm always getting waylaid but it's never ever planned.

Now the barman's smashing bottles in the noisy bottle bin!
So I'm sorry that you spoke at me and I didn't take it in...

Mortal enemy

You're the fox that's running for your life — and I'm the hound.
I'm the knife that slices your Achilles, drops you to the ground.
I'm exhaustion, I'm insomnia. I'm the reason you don't sleep.
I'm the cause, the reason I'm the anguish when you weep.

You don't make the decisions — I'm the one in charge.
I'm your abuser, your killer, a criminal at large.
I'm the disease in your veins, the clot in your heart.
I'm your internal demon, ripping you apart.

I'm the doubt and the panic, again and again.
Your foe. Your thorn. Your enemy. I own you.

......I'm your brain.

Do sheep get heavier in the rain?

Do sheep get heavier in the rain?
Why don't they make pork curry?
What was that odd kid's name from school?
Why do these things make me worry?

Why don't giraffes have vocal cords?
What time does Maccies close?
Or is it 24 hours now?
There's bloody loads of those!

Could I beat a baboon in a fight?
Why is Mario so short?
Why don't moths just fly at the sun?
Why did I think that thought?

If Atlas held the world up,
How did he find time to eat?
What happened to Cardi A?
Who keeps pissing on the seat?

Why does this always happen
When I get up for a wee?
Switch off, you arsehole of a brain —
It's half past fucking 3.

Box theory.

I'd like you to imagine that you have a couple of tasks.
Just a bit of tidying up – Not a massive ask.
20 boxes, all the same that you need to do today,
There's an empty room the exact size, not far away.

You'd work out the dimensions of the boxes and the room,
And tidy them neatly away with zero existential doom.
After that you're free to go and have a little chill.
Now imagine it this way, indulge me if you will.

You've got to do it all again, but this time instead,
You've read the plan 4 times but it's not sticking in your head.
Your boxes are not box shaped, they're loads of random sizes,
And someone is distracting you with jump scares and surprises.

The cupboard is full up of shit you have to get out first,
It's heaving with things lodged in tight like it's about to burst.
Now imagine the cupboard is at the top of the hill,
And you're at the bottom, that knob head distracting still.

You're still unsure, and lost the paper where the task was written,
Then the prick distracting you pulls out a tiny kitten…
That is pretty much the best way that I can explain,
What the fuck it's like to have an ADHD brain.
So sorry if we tire quick or if we seem quite lazy,
We're trying to keep up but our brains are fucking crazy!

I wonder what it is?

I wonder what it is? I wonder what it is?
Brain in overdrive like it's a question in a quiz
Excitement doesn't really ever rear its twitchy head.
But the waiting is frustrating, like a wasp trapped in a shed.

Why isn't it here? Why isn't it here?
They said by noon it would arrive, in writing, loud and clear!
I'm sitting by the window like an eager little pup
But now they're 8 minutes late, I wish they'd hurry up!

It's taking far too long! It's taking far too long!
And now I'm double checking, did I get the timings wrong?
It wouldn't be the first time that I messed up which day.
I've triple checked the time again… it's definitely today!

A van has just arrived!! A van has just arrived!
Hopefully it's for me, have they brought me my surprise?
No that's the wrong house mate, the deliveries for me..
That must've just been something else for number 93..

Finally it's here! Finally it's here!!
I feel like I'm Andy and I've just got Buzz Lightyear!
I don't remember buying this, somehow I never do..
Another box of random shit — courtesy of Temu…

Neuro domino

"I'm sorry, babe, we need to talk — I hope I don't sound harsh,
Your ADHD affects me too — your brain's a boggy marsh.
I don't mean that to sound real bad, I hope you understand,
It's like being stuck in a lift with a really shit brass band.

All these noises happening, your 'projects' all unfinished —
You papered half the wall last week then your focus diminished.
I ask if you can wash the pots, you start and that's all great,
But when I came back later, you were painting next door's gate!

This behaviour is unbearable — I'm starting to believe
That I can't do this anymore — maybe I should leave.
I could go to my parents — just a week or so, you'll see.
The house would be an utter mess if it were not for me.

I want you to support me more, that's what I want — it's true.
I'd just like some extra help... is that something you can do?"

"Babe?"

"Babe? Is that something you can do?"

"What?"

Cunts.

I know a cunt who falls asleep as soon as he lies down.
I know a cunt who is a proper man about the town.
I know a cunt who's not depressed, how's that even fair?
Yet I walk into a room and forget why I'm even there.

I know a cunt who gets on well in social situations.
I know a cunt who always gets off at the right tube station.
I know a cunt who can take criticisms on the chin.
Yet I have to read a book 3 times before the words sink in.

I know a cunt who talks to random people in a bar!
I know a cunt who jokes but doesn't take things way too far.
I know a cunt who stands proud and can poise the perfect posture.
Yet I can't do anything without feeling like an imposter.

I know a cunt who doesn't get anxious or over zealous.
I know a cunt who can see folks have fun and not get jealous.
I know a cunt who doesn't have daily battles with their brain.
Whilst I sit here wondering if I am going insane.

Reaching.

There's a light at the end of the tunnel, I know cos I can see.
It's only barely visible but it's flickering at me..
There's a light at the end of the tunnel, but honestly, I don't care.
It's a long way in the distance and I doubt I can make it there..

There's a light at the end of the tunnel, shining, making itself known.
But I bet it's crowded over there, I prefer it here, alone..
There's a light at the end of the tunnel, or so it's just been said,
By the voice that I keep hearing — on repeat — inside my head.

The voice that tells me "end my life" and fills my soul with fear.
The same voice that says "keep fighting" and makes me persevere.
So if this voice I'm hearing is now making contradictions,
Why should I even listen and let it help make my decisions?..

There's a light at the end of the tunnel and although it's not that clear,
Myself and millions more of us are slowly crawling near!
We're doing it together, just one step at a time,
Until, in the not far distance you can see the finish line!

There's a light at the end of the tunnel, and I've not made it yet.
But with support from others I have altered my mindset.
There's a light at the end of the tunnel, but before I make it there,
I've stopped and turned around and into darkness I now stare.

But not in the way I did before, this time I take a stand,
And reach back into darkness offering my helping hand.

Darkness isn't forever. It can feel like it is sometimes, and sometimes the finish line can seem far away. Please know that there are people always looking back and reaching out a hand, whether it be a friend, an empath or a professional, help is available. Unfortunately they can't find you if you hide in the dark. Make yourself visible and the light at the end of the tunnel becomes visible too. Take one big, uncomfortable leap in the direction that seems hopeless and grab the hand reaching for you. Be brave, be strong and be kind to yourself. X

Plancellation.

"Morning mate, how's the fam? I've got something to say.
I can't do tonight anymore — can we do another day?"
"The reason? Well... my cat got sick and I need to babysit."
"Come on, mate — don't be like that. No, it's not bullshit."

"I have an essay to hand in... I've not started it yet."
"Erm yeah, I go to college — can't believe you'd forget."
"My grandma died last night... and my grandad's almost done."
"It's a shame, I was excited — tonight would've been fun."

"Okay, okay, I'm sorry mate — you're right, she died last year.
I'll be honest from now on, yeah? Undoubtedly sincere.
Today's just been one of those — a battle with my brain,
A storm inside my head — it's exhausting. It's a drain."

"So that's the real excuse, mate. No more lying from me now."
"Oh... also, I can't do Saturday. Why? I'm fighting Pacquiao."

Plancelled on.

"Hiya mate, family's good thanks — yeah sure, what's on your mind?
We rescheduled this last week too — your dog was going blind?.."
What is your excuse this time? I hope your cat pulls through?
You're not gonna babysit? Come on... seriously? You?

An essay, hey? That can't be right — the term's not started yet.
You got kicked off your course last year, it made you dead upset.
Your grandma died again? Really? She died four times last year.
I'm sorry if I've got that wrong — you've not been very clear.

Yeah, it is a shame you've cancelled, mate — the reason's sketchy though.
Like when your gran died last time... then I saw her in Tesco.
That's better, mate, and thank you for being honest now with me.
I get your situation — it's not done maliciously.

Take care mate, look after yourself — we'll rearrange next week...
Mate! — you can't even box. That excuse is weak!!

Request pending.

I'll do it in a minute. A statement overused,
It comes out automatically. A sentence I've abused.
I'd like to say my intentions are pure when it gets said.
But then begins the battle in my overthinking head.

My brain's already juggling 7 more complexities.
And adding more fuel to that fire brings perplexities.
So "I'll do it in a minute" can't be taken literally.
Take it like you would take an elaborate simile.

But rest assured that your request is now being considered,
I just can't confirm when a result will be delivered.

The Scenic route.

There's nothing quite like driving around,
The Purring engine is the only sound,
The wind blowing through your hair.
The scenery is beyond compare.

Not a care in the world, just you and the road.
Your brain is switched to relax mode.
Then suddenly right out of the blue,
A man comes and interrupts you.

"Sorry sir, get off, no fuss.
And the bastard kicks you off the bus!

Don't give up giving up.

I have realised something over the last year or two,
I'm doing something often that I just don't want to do.
I know I've had some vices in the past that ain't been great.
But this realisation has just hit me like a freight.

I used to smoke from 15 to the age of twenty six.
Then cannabis and alcohol to name another fix.
I tried to quit my life for fuck sake, I wouldn't be around,
Then you wouldn't be reading this, and I'd be in the ground.

I've quit these things, I had the strength, I can do it again.
I just need to prepare for all the heartache and the pain.
The heartache and the pain I'd be avoiding though, a perk!
Cos the thing I really wanna quit is turning up to work.

It's not that I don't like the place or all the people here,
They pay me well, they've got my back, I wanna make that clear.
But getting up at 5am to do a twelve hour shift,
Or working on twelve hour nights, it gets me fucking miffed.

Cos if I had those hours back to use for me instead,
I'd probably waste them all somehow or just go back to bed..

Suicidal sympathies.

Another name goes on the list. Ryan, thirty two.
We could have figured it out man. We were here for you.
You had the world inside your palm, you were kind and clever.
Now you're gone you've left a hole, it'll be with us forever.

Another friend who's gone too soon, a friend darkness devoured.
I've had a fight with Jamie, he said you were a coward.
And even though I know, if you could man, you'd regret it.
But I know what the darkness does.
I love you man.

I get it.

Forty

forty years have passed while I've been trying to fit in.
Like a chameleon, changing the colour of my skin.
Seeking recognition, wearing masks to hide the shame.
Watching people flourish, wishing I could do the same.

Forty years have passed and I still wear the same disguise,
It's like a real part of me, shielding the lies.
But changing who you are is just a way to try and cope.
And if you aren't the real you, then how do we find hope?

Forty years have passed and I'm finally understanding.
We don't have to conform to what society's demanding.
I've faced the dark, I've faced the pain, now finally I see.
I'll never know myself unless I just let me be me.

Dead tired.

I didn't get to sleep last night, I laid awake instead.
The same nothing and everything, floating round my head.
Sometimes I wonder if it's even worth going to bed.
But then my alarm screams and I could sleep like I was dead!

When the mask is broken.

My life revolved around the art of pleasing everyone.
Wearing someone else's skin, just to get along.
A master of deflection and trying to seem more formal,
But I don't want that, that makes you forgettably normal.

So I parade around this world wearing my big disguise.
I've been wearing it so long now, I'm corrupted by its guise.
I settled in at first inside the ruse I'd had to foster.
Is this me? If so, why do I feel like an imposter?

Darkness pecked away at my now flailing imitation.
But light poured in through splintered holes, bringing a revelation.
And through the cracks that formed upon the mask I always wore.
I learned I was mistaken about what I'm living for.

Cos when you find you're stuck between survival or suppression,
You leave yourself no room to breathe, harbouring depression.
You'll always have a third choice, one that's valiant and true.
Don't try to be somebody else, there's nothing wrong with you.

Proverb problems.

A watched kettle never boils or so the saying goes.
But I can never wait that long, I'll take your word I s'pose.
A bad workman blames his tools, another odd quotation.
I've every tool for every job but that was yesterday's fixation.

Good things come to those who wait, well that one isn't fair!
I can't wait for long unless you strap me to the chair!
A picture is worth a thousand words, another thing they say.
Well then picture yourself smiling and having a nice day.

The place.

I visited a place once and came back a different man.
I've been back more since then and it keeps changing who I am.

In this place I'm treated like I am a VIP
It's cordoned off so nobody can use it except me.

I leave a piece of me behind with every visitation.
I keep getting called back but I don't want an invitation!

Last time I returned from there I didn't recognise myself.
It totally obliterated my fragile mental health.

This place has exclusivity. Only I'm allowed to go.
It's asked me back again and I don't know how to say no.

The place is called depression and it causes so much pain.
It's located in the darkest corner deep inside my brain.

Just a word.

Depression - just 1 simple word. 3 syllables, 10 letters..
A single word that holds so much, can anger and upset us.
To people on the other side, depression's just a word,
The lack of understanding of its power is absurd.

I think you need to feel it first before you understand it.
Once you feel what it can do, you'll get it, it demands it.
A word of endless meanings, each one soaked in hurt.
It drags you from your place of light and slams you in the dirt.

To be back on the other side where ignorance is bliss.
Where depression is still just a word, no sign of the abyss.
Don't hate those on the other side if they don't understand.
Just be ready if they slip the fence and need a helping hand.

Cos if I had the choice then I'd pick ignorance too,
Depression would just be a word, not like it is to you..

Boulders.

The possible's impossible,
Rationality? irrational.
The wrong idea is the right idea,
Bad feelings come so natural.

Nothing is straightforward when you're battling with depression.
Heightened states of sadness, stress, hopelessness and aggression.
You're constantly exhausted, each problem feels like boulders.
Pushing you down consistently, a huge weight atop your shoulders.

Each boulder though, has options and ways to make it disappear.
But when they're piled up, none of those options are clear.
But take your smallest boulder and pay it a bit of time.
One boulder isn't anything with your mountain to climb.

Smash one small boulder, then another —you'll soon see,
The other boulders lighten as you move on to boulder three.
There is no correct order, smash the easiest few first,
You don't need to smash them orderly from easiest to worst.

Some boulders need some help to lift but help is all around.
Wave your flag, say you need help then someone will be found.
You won't float out of darkness — there's no magic, no quick fix.
But light creeps in through cracks between the problems you can pick.

You're not out yet — but listen: you're not where you began.
A few small boulders broken. A few steps in your plan.
So take a breath. Stay standing. Let the mountain slowly shift.
Each boulder moved is proof enough — you haven't lost your grip.

Sweet restraint.

Did you know there's people that live amongst you and me,
Who opens up a bag of sweets and just eats 2 or 3?
What kind of sorcery is this, where do they find resolve?
Were they trained up by shaolin monks? Was wizardry involved?
I know that I can't compete with that level of composure,
I can't stop until they're gone, I guess I need closure?..
I'll blame just about anyone to take the heat off me.
But there's only 1 person at fault...

It's my ADHD!!

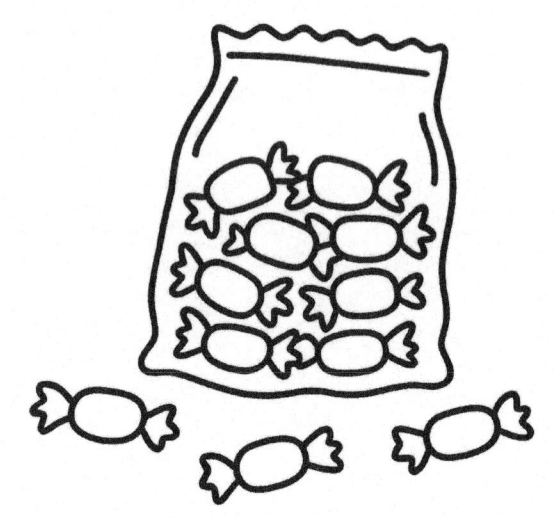

Listening, not hearing.

The worst trait as a neuro-d, is listening but not hearing.
We look and seem like we're following but it's not how it's appearing.
I see you making words and I'm engrossed in the conversation.
The words go in but come back out whilst my brain takes a vacation.

It makes it ten times worse sometimes when I ask you to repeat.
To find I'd spaced out once again, a double, neuro-treat...

Give him a chance!

I learnt I was neurodivergent in twenty twenty-four.
A diagnosis I wish so much that I knew years before.
I thought I'd write this letter now to help you understand —
Not everything you want to do is gonna go as planned.

Relationships, behaviour, raw emotion, pain and doubt.
Lack of concentration — sometimes you will feel burnt out.
When you begin to notice that you just aren't fitting in,
When you feel like you're an alien in someone else's skin,

There's a reason for that, fella — you're not wired like the rest.
Don't beat yourself, okay? Just try and do your best.
'Cos you have a condition that affects your concentration,
It can make you feel vulnerable in any situation.

I know how determined you are — I was just the same,
But determination turned to doubt when I had nothing to blame.
I guess I'm trying to say I know you better than you do.
I'd like you to be prepared for the things life throws at you.

So I hope this letter helps you find a little extra might,
Avoid the darkness I found, gain the will to fight.
Understand, when things go wrong, you're not always to blame.
I thought I was broken — I don't want you to feel the same.

My intentions aren't to influence any of your choices,
Please know that you don't always have to listen to the voices.
Sometimes they'll be your best friend, then others they're foe.
Either way, they're here to stay — a mental cargo.

And finally, kid, you have to look after your mental health.
Keep smiling, be honest, and just be kind to yourself.
I hope that you become the man that you deserve to be.
It's time for me to go now.

Goodbye, younger me.

Riding the Darkness.

Darkness has arrived again, I didn't feel it coming.
It sneaks in when you least expect. It's dull, incessant drumming.
Don't take me to that place again, I beg don't make me go.
There must be some kind of mistake, just say it isn't so!

I've done the things they told me to, Everything they said.
I haven't had a drink for months, I've not forcefully bled.
I'm walking outdoors every day, I'm getting enough rest.
And if there's something troubling me I get it off my chest.

Have I forgotten to take my meds? Could I have missed a dose?
Is it my imagination? Is it not really getting close?
It could be something else I feel, not darkness, just a migraine?
I feel it in my whole head though, not a "just behind the eye pain."

This anxiety is killing me, it's making me unsteady.
If you're coming back then hurry up! Get on with it already.
I'll accept you're back for now, I'll open up my arms.
I'm more prepared for you this time, so come on in, no qualms.

I won't resist you anymore, I'm unlocking the doors.
You won't defeat me darkness,
you're mine — I'm not yours!

The voice.

You're boring now stop talking, you're not the boss of me!
I don't care if you approve of what we had tonight for tea.
So what? We missed the gym again, it's really not an issue.
Oh, now you're all upset, boohoo, let me grab a tissue!

Stop trying to control me, why'd you think you rule the roost?
You said you'd stop complaining. You promised, made a truce.
I don't know why you think that you can make the big decisions.
Just leave it man, I'm tired and just watching television.

Oh there you go again putting your beak where it's not wanted!
You're everywhere I go, it's like I'm being fucking haunted..
Sometimes I honestly think I'd be better if you're dead..
Do normal people argue with the voices in their head?

I cried today.

I cried today, it just happened, I couldn't hold it in.
A storm inside me, so immense it spilled over the brim.
I used to bottle it all up, emotions, pain and grief.
Like a rabid dog inside a cage, begging for its release.

Alcohol and drugs had formed a tomb around my pain.
The numbness that came with it wreaked havoc with my brain.
My darkness grew so big it burst the walls off of its crypt.
Spewing out its fury like a tiger that's been whipped.

I felt I'd been smashed to pieces, impossible to mend.
I knew what I had to do. I knew this was the end.
The world looks really different from atop a fire escape.
It somehow felt liberating, the plan falling into shape.

The sun, red as blood as it was forced out of the sky.
Like a tribute to my twisted soul, the wind whispered goodbye,
I watched as darkness poured in like a tropical monsoon.
Swallowing the dregs of light then spitting out the moon.

I climbed over the railing, calm, I didn't feel the fear.
Like a tragedy unfolding — The ending drawing near.
A tear escaped my eye and trickled softly down my face.
Mapping out its course as if it's searching for its place.

Another tear retraced its tracks forcing it to drop.
Tear drops turned to waterfalls I felt they'd never stop.
For the first time in a long time I'd allowed myself to feel.
It ripped me from my nightmare and things actually seemed real.

Darkness nearly snuffed me out just like it did the sun.
But the sun will fight back soon like everyday since time begun.
Had I just experienced an epiphany?
It felt like the universe had just acknowledged me.

That day was the first day of the rest of my life.
I asked for help, not for me but my gorgeous son and wife.
I set off down the winding road intent on my revival.
A path full of life's battles try to deny me my survival.

I've recently accepted that I'll always walk this road.
It's hard but I'm devoted to this chance I've been bestowed.
With very little effort things were falling back in line.
And an understanding that the healing will take time.

I feel I own this person now where my soul resides
I have good days, I have bad days like the changing of the tides.
Sometimes still when darkness calls I proudly admit I cry.
I allow myself to feel it now, it helps, give it a try.

Meanwhile, Dave... (Neurodivimmerick)

There once was a neuro called Dave,
Who decided he needed a shave.
Forgot where he's going,
And boarded a Boeing,
Now he's in Crete at a rave...

The cat's eyes.

"He's doing it again — the fifteenth time this week.
He always gets that twitchy leg when I'm trying to sleep.
As if the thunderous snoring wasn't frustrating enough,
Last time I tried to wake him, I ended up sleeping rough!

He put me in the garden in the middle of the night,
Then that Tom from two doors down showed up to start a fight.
Forget it — I'll just go downstairs and sleep on his clean clothes.
I think he really loves me getting hair all over those.

I don't understand the choices that these humans make.
He keeps on walking in the room, stops and shouts "fuck sake!"
It really makes me wonder what he's coming in here for.
He's coming back again — it must be thirteen times or more.

He looks like he's upset, so I will snuggle on his knee.
I hope his twitchy legs don't shake me off the settee!
Oh no — that online shop again, he's just about to pay!
He's always buying random stuff — I sleep most of the day.

Yes, I may be a lazy, needy, unapologetic cat,
But I'd much rather this life than to run around like that!
The best thing about the human, though, I really have to say:
He feeds me — then forgets. I've eaten seven times today!!"

The ADHD control room.

Good morning ladies and gents, and hello — my name's Brenda.
Today we will walk through the daily ADHD agenda.
We've work at 8 till 4 p.m, then we need to get some shopping.
Gym if we've got time left, and tea's pork with cheese sauce topping.

Very straightforward day today — idiot level: moron.
We need a partner too. Bonus points if you procure one.
So work's just five miles away, the commute takes fifteen minutes.
Set an alarm for 7 a.m. — you can snooze once, that's the limit.

Fine then, just ignore the alarm until seven thirty-six.
Calm down — you're running aimlessly, throwing panic in the mix.
Good! Nine minutes from your bed to the car — wait? An icy screen?
We didn't account for this at all — it should've been foreseen!

Window down — head poking out - blowers on full blast.
The time is seven fifty-two — you're on the road at last.
Stick to the speed limit where you can. Today's limit's ninety-two.
Luckily the ice acts like a shield, obscuring you from view.

Now tank it down the bypass — nearly there, you're doing great.
Aaaaaand stop — you made it, you're at work... eleven minutes late.
Alright, it's time to sneak in. Head down now — that's it, good.
Now play it cool... or tell Dianne your views on Robin Hood.

Okay, it's lunchtime — let us see what you threw in your bag.
Bugger — wrong bag again. That's not last night's kebab.
We'll pop up to the canteen and see what they have to eat.
Oh, it's pork. Well, that's a shame — good job you like meat.

Okay, head down, three hours to go... is Sam giving you the eye?
Oh — you're shaking the desk again. Sorry, Sam. Silly guy.
Work's over. Now head to the car — let's get the shopping done.
We need milk, bread, Coco Pops, and spearmint chewing gum.

Eerm... let's park over these two spots. That's it. Now let's get to it.
We MUST avoid the middle aisle, your compulsion won't get through it.
Okay, that's done — and luckily we got all we went for...
We also bought two planters, and somehow, a hacksaw.

I'm not sure that we needed that. We don't have full control.
We still have time to hit the gym — let's hit our 'fitness goal'.
Okay, there's lots of ladies here — let's turn on the charm.
NO NO — you don't say lovely bum whilst holding her arm!

It's okay, sometimes we struggle to avoid misadventure...
Besides, she smiled and giggled — his next potential venture?
Okay, get washed, we're going home — we're getting pretty hungry.
Can you feel that, boys and girls? His tummy's getting grumbly!

Okay, who wants to do the bit where he cooks his pork for tea?
Oh no — we lost control again... he's ordered KFC.

I'd like to take my brain out!

I'd like to take my brain out,
Give it a little shake.
Ask it why it won't shut up
Switch off for goodness sake.

I'd like to take my brain out,
Ask what it's playing at.
Stop making me say stupid stuff
You've made me look a twat.

I'd like to take my brain out,
I'm trying to be jolly!
Boot it over next door's fence,
A Roberto Carlos volley!

I'd like to take my brain out.
I think it must be faulty
I said I'm on a diet,
Why'd you order chicken balti?

I'd like to take my brain out,
Store in a safe and lock the door.
Why does it run round like a
 hyperactive Labrador!

I'd like to take my brain out,
I'd stick it in the wash.
But if I didn't have a brain
I suppose I wouldn't be Josh.

The persistent optimist.

Today it will be different, today we will try again.
Today we're fighting back once more, going against the grain.
We've learned from yesterday's disarray, we'll get it right this time.
With much more structured plans in place, we've moved the boundary line.

The blueprints of our new approach are totally foolproof.
This optimistic outlook couldn't be further from the truth.
When something starts to go wrong or you find your plan is flawed.
You take the issues personally, you feel like a fraud.

You've failed again, you've fucked this up, you falter once more.
Now remaining tasks change form from job to mundane chore.
Some days I can't overcome the feeling of deflation.
Good intentions turn to dust, lining your damnation.

A big neurodivergent trait is called self-deprivation.
Made worse with every hour of harsh procrastination
Another trait we have though is strong resiliency.
A skill that we've adapted with robust brilliancy.

We step back and take a look at all the troubles in our way.
And we know that we can fuck it up again another day..

Grief is a funny old thing.

I find humour in my pain, my darkness and my dread.
If I didn't then I wouldn't be anything but dead.
It doesn't mean when someone dies I laugh the pain away.
It lingers on and stops me, keeping my demons at bay.

I don't find it amusing when I throw a fit of rage!
Shouting every nasty word as I escape my cage.
But when I look back later and I'm calm and level headed,
I pick apart the problem, finding humour that's embedded.

So when you make a fuck-up that you'll carry to the grave,
Don't obsess on who it hurts, or how you didn't behave.
Look a little deeper — you might also come to find,
That little bit of humour that stopped me losing my mind.

Life.

The thing that grinds me down the most about this life malarkey,
Being born into a system, designed by an oligarchy.
A system that we have to follow from the age of four.
Being prepped to join the rest, a politician's whore.

You have to work, you need a house, it's money, money, money,
Inflation on our basic needs for profit just ain't funny!
We're governed by private school toffs, corrupt beyond belief.
Meticulously prepped to be a liar and a thief.

Rich business men above, pulling strings like puppeteers,
Whilst people cannot feed their kids, their bills are in arrears.
50% of all money is owned by the super rich,
Thats 1% of people making me and you their bitch.

So as you leave your house at 5 am to get to work.
You're just lining the pockets of a brutal, selfish jerk.
Labouring for 14 hours a day, worked to the bone,
Just to earn enough so you can buy your empty home.

These ghosts control the people who effectively control you.
And you're just a pawn to help the turning of the screw.
Political corruption brazenly gets overlooked,
The elderly are freezing as we're forcefully dry fucked.

You're fuelled by propaganda, you're made to feel scared.
Mould you into dependency, get you all prepared.
And please don't get me wrong, I'm not hounding the successful,
Who've worked to earn their riches, who've lived the hard and stressful.

It's the monsters at the top whose only want in life is power.
Heartless men who live on greed atop their ivory tower.
To them you're just a number. Filed into a line.
To me you are a human, complex with beauty in design.

Stood next to the super rich and stripped back to your soul,
The differences are glaring — like your motives and your goal.
'Cos if you had their money you could almost guarantee,
That everyone would benefit...

Except for them maybe...

Thank you.

A few years back when I was low It hadn't crossed my mind that I could write poetry or publish a book. In fact, last month it also hadn't occurred to me either.

I was told during the depths of my depression that I needed to talk more. I did talk more and it did help. Now I advocate talking when someone is down. I like to be open with friends and family about everything now. Too open sometimes apparently...

Some days I can't think of anything I'd rather not do than talk to people. Some days I just need to be with myself. Talking can be emotionally tiring. I will write things down instead though. I like to write poetry because it helps me to feel my emotions properly and process my thoughts at the same time. The notes stored on my phone are an ever growing collection of short stories, poems, jokes, feelings and the general random 3am bollocks that I think up instead of sleeping.

I guess I'm really just saying that you can do the things that you think you can't. This book is proof. I still get low, I think I always will, but I have some tools to deal with it now. That's because i talked. Let yourself be seen and be kind to yourself.
Thank you. Josh x

Talk to someone, anyone.

"Hi... My name is,K-K-Keith... What's yours?"

"Hey baby — Crystal." [long pause...]
"What you doing, baby? How is your day?"

"Eeeeerm... Not much... It's been ok."

"You shy, Keithy? I don't bite."

"Y-yeah... Yeah a bit... It's alright."

"So, Keithy, baby — What would you like me to do?"

"Well... C-C-Crystal...
Just tell me everything's going to be ok.
Tell me I'm ok... That I'm enough.
Tell me I'm not having an existential crisis. Tell me, Crystal...

Then let me lay my head on your knee...
And cry a bit.... W-W-Whilst you stroke my hair.
And hush me to sleep...
Th-th-that's it R-r-really..."

Eulogy.

Come on in — you may as well sit in the front two pews.
Yes, this is the service for... a Mr, erm... Andrews.
We're gathered here today to remember the life of a man.
A man with lots of heart. A helping hand, where he can.

At eighteen, unsure of his path, he worked as a milkman.
Before joining the army and serving in Afghanistan.
Private Andrews was a soldier — for just four years of his life.
Then moved back to his hometown, where he met his late wife.

Returning to do milk rounds again, he slowly settled down.
He bought a cottage near the park, on the edge of town.
He worked hard, kept to himself... until three years ago,
When Susan lost her long battle — leaving him all alone.

Mr Andrew's eventually... surrendered to his grief.
You're gone, but not forgotten.
Rest in peace.

To Keith.

I tried.

I tried today–
Or at least, I tried.

I mean,
I tried to try today,
Is what I tried to say.

So today,
I tried to try.

But i didn't

Try again tomorrow..

The tree.

A tree stood in the distance — beautifully unique.
Its branches carved their own paths, shaping its physique.
You cannot hear its story, but you know it's lived it well,
Silently rooted to its spot — secrets it just can't tell.

How many lives has this tree seen? How many stopped to gaze?
How many creatures sheltered here over its many days?
The beauty of this tree, you see, is it's not like any other —
Shaped purely by nature's hand, with the love of a mother.

Its aim from when it was a seed — grow towards the sun,
While rooting its security, since the day its life begun.
The freedom bestowed upon her crafted something exclusive,
No external influence or need to be inclusive.

It's unapologetically the shape it chose to be —
Nothing to conform to, no guidance to agree.
So why is it this tree, a consequence of liberty,
Is not an example of how we're supposed to be?

An incredible masterpiece birthed by independence,
Devoid of indoctrination and with no form of ascendance.
Yet 'free souls' living life the way they want to be
Have vulnerabilities due to lack of conformity?

So whilst everyone fights it out to be exemplary and seen —
I let my branches do their thing...

It's the happiest I've been.

Flipped!

"AAAARGH! Tania you absolute melt, do some fucking work!
How the fuck is it appropriate to teach Alan to twerk?
Alan, don't try and defend please you're annoying as it is,
Flirting around the drink machine like a pair of fucking kids!

Oh I know I'm not your boss and I can't tell you what to do,
But you've got me to the point where I'm about to go kung fu!
And if I was your boss you wouldn't fucking be here,
Without a doubt I would've sacked your lazy arse last year.

Oh, the boss is out the office now, welcome to the show Stu!
A triple amputee dead badger has more charisma than you.
You're not fit to manage, you're a lazy fucking prick.
We all know you got the job because you suck a dick!

And whilst we're on the topic of you fuckers sucking cock.
Sally's keeping quiet! Oi sally! Come and join the flock.
You bunch of useless twats are the epitome of lazy,
The fact someone employed you 4 is totally crazy.

And Doug you big old hairy prick, you're actually ok..
Although you smell like ass, death and cheese combined today!"
"Oooh thats better.."

Afterwards.

Throughout my life I've been living under the immense weight,
Of trying to impress folk with the roles I imitate.
Normal me did not fit in so well when school began,
So much so that 'fitting in' became my main game-plan.

I got good at being who I thought I had to be,
So much so that I forgot what it's like to be me.
Discovering I had ADHD was significant news.
It gave a bit of context to the partying and booze.

It's not that I don't want to own the person that I was,
It's knowing that there may have been an underlying cause.
Addiction, impulsivity, and struggling with attention,
Are traits that are common in our neuro-spicy nation.

Another trait is self-destruction and a hatred for oneself,
Which starts to impact heavily on your mental health.
So now I can be kinder to myself, or at least try.
The grey clouds vanish from your mind, leaving just blue sky.

Understanding means that I get off of my own back.
Focussing on other things and getting life on track.
The biggest challenge now is that I have to realise.
Who I really am under my forty-year disguise…

Hard to explain.

It's waking up tired of waking up.
It's forgetting how to want something.
It's brushing your teeth
just to say you did something today.

It's staring at a text for four hours
and feeling too broken to reply —
even though you care.
Even though they matter.

It's being the life of the party once,
and now being the "Sorry I can't" that fades from invite lists.
It's hearing "Just reach out"
and wondering how to scream
when your voice is underwater
and your arms are tired of waving.

It's not wanting to die —
it's not wanting to live like this.

It's knowing something's wrong
but feeling too lost to ask for directions.

It's dead weight.

On your chest.

In your head.

Behind your eyes.

And you carry it anyway,
because some stubborn part of you
refuses to let go of the idea
that there might still be light
on the other side of the dark.

If You're Struggling.

If anything in this book hit a little too hard — or if you find yourself struggling in silence — please know you're not alone. Life can be unbearably heavy sometimes. I've been there, and I know how loud the quiet can get.

Asking for help isn't weakness — it's survival. It's strength in the rawest form.

If you're in the UK and need someone to talk to, here are some places you can reach out to:

- **Samaritans – 116 123 (free, 24/7)**

- **Mind – 0300 123 3393 or text 86463 (Mon-Fri, 9am-6pm)**

- **SHOUT – Text 'SHOUT' to 85258 (free, 24/7)**

- **NHS Mental Health Helpline – Call 111 and press option 2**

Wherever you are, search for mental health helplines in your country — someone will be there. Someone will listen. You matter.

Take care of your weird, wonderful self.

Printed in Great Britain
by Amazon